Spot in the Dark

# Spot in the Dark

Beth Gylys

THE OHIO STATE UNIVERSITY PRESS • Columbus

Library of Congress Cataloging-in-Publication Data

Gylys, Beth.
      Spot in the dark / Beth Gylys.
            p. cm.
ISBN 0-8142-0981-5 (cloth : alk. paper) — ISBN 0-8142-9057-4 (cd-rom)
I. Man-woman relationships—Poetry. 2. Interpersonal relations—Poetry. 3. Soli-
tude—Poetry. I. Title.
PS3607.Y58S68 2004
811'.6—dc22

                              2004020840

Paper (ISBN: 978-0-8142-5723-4)
Cover by Dan O'Dair.
Type set in Adobe Bembo

This book is dedicated in memory of my beloved, deceased grandmothers:
Angeline Sutton and Anna Kowalski.

# Contents

## IV

# Acknowledgments

Many helped to bring this book into being. Jeff Worley, Diana Hume George, Jon Schofer and Michael Walls gave invaluable comments on early drafts of this manuscript. Ellen Bryant Voigt helped me to find the pulse of poems in section II. Thanks to members of my writers groups at George's and in upstate New York who commented on early drafts of some of these poems—thanks especially to Cathy Carlisi for her keen insights and good spirit and to Nancy Whitelaw for being such a generous host. Thanks to Michael Opperman, Dan Welcher, Jim Cummins, and Nkanyiso Mpofu for inspiration and support, and to Rodger Moody for his grace and unflagging support and for encouraging me to wait. Thanks also to Andrew Hudgins for guidance and for choosing the manuscript as a finalist and to David Citino for making the final selection. I also thank Georgia State University for financial and professional support and the MacDowell Colony for wonderful food and time to muse.

I am deeply grateful to the editors of the journals where these poems first appeared.

- *32 Poems:* "Wheels Inside Wheels"
- *Blue Moon Review:* "Pilgrimage"
- *Caffeine Destiny:* "To One Who Can't Leave"
- *Canary River:* "Another Departure" and "With a Woman"
- *Cimarron:* "My Doggy Self"
- *Connecticut Poetry Review:* "Explanations for Distraction" and "The Art of Schmoozing"
- *Good Foot:* "Lyric Melancholia" and "Spot in the Dark"
- *Kenyon Review:* "No News Here"
- *Pierian Springs Review:* "Alone, Open Road"
- *Poetry Kanto:* "The Letter I Sent to My Mother," "My Former Lover Said He Was Tired," and "Me and You and an Oh"
- *Poet Lore:* "If Only" and "Nowhere Fast"
- *Puerto del Sol:* "Winter, Erie, PA"
- *Terminus:* "Boardwalk and Bach" and "The Distance of Motion"
- *Southern Review:* "Winter Preparations"
- *Wind:* "Falling in Love Again" and "Hands Full of Nothing"
- *Word:* "Friend of a Friend of a"

Also thanks to the editor of the anthology *On the Shores of Lake Erie,* where the following poems are forthcoming, for permission to print them here: "Teaching Composition in Erie, Pennsylvania" and "Again."

## Spot in the Dark

In love, he bought himself a laser gun,
and used its spot of light to tease his dog.
She lived three hours away, but they talked each night.
Why did he always find these women, dark,
a hot flash in a pan of trouble? "Sick,"
he murmured, "I must be really sick." His love

twisted in his gut. "You're not in love,"
his ex snorted when he told her. They'd gone
to lunch the week before. "It's just a sick
infatuation." Nights, he'd take his dog
and walk the graveyard. The breeze, the bluish dark
would calm his aching heart. Why did the night

appease him so? He thought about the night
six months before, how fast he'd fallen in love.
He met her in a dive, a smoky, dark
hole of a place, where locals liked to gun
their engines. He'd ordered fries, a foot-long dog.
She'd been there with some friends. "It wasn't sick,"

he said out loud, remembered her eyes, "not sick
at all," the way he'd wanted her that night.
They drank and talked until he heard his dog
outside. "I better go. I'd really love
to know you more." They hadn't even begun,
he realized. She scrawled her number in the dark.

Now he lived for moments in the dark
with her beside him: skin, wine, music,
lips. She had to live in Michigan.
She had to be the type that wants a knight
in shining armor, that looks to every love
to save her from herself. She tried to dog

him into moving. "My job, the house, the dog—
how can I move?" he pleaded in the dark,
the cordless phone, lifeline to his love.
It didn't matter what he said. How sick
he'd feel when they hung up. Even the night
seemed unforgiving, his heart a loaded gun.

He heard his dog whining in the dark,
turned on the laser gun and fenced the night.
He wondered if love would always make him sick.

## Fallen in Love Again,

they try to reinvent the whole thing,
so it's not boring. "You make me feel
like balloons full of helium," he says.
"Like the ocean but it's breathing,"
she responds. When he touches her,
his fingers are small portions of light
meeting small portions of light inside her.
"What are you thinking?" he asks.
"Of jack-o-lanterns and big smiley faces.
Isn't that stupid?" Instead of wine and candles,
they drink Jack Daniels with a lava lamp.
He makes her Rice Krispie treats
and paints his fingernails bright blue.
She gives him an old pair of socks
from her grandfather. One has a hole in the toe,
the other, in the heel. "He wore these
till his death," she says soberly. He hangs them
above his mantle. "You divide me like the red sea,"
she tells him after making love. He replies:
"Moving inside your body, I feel like
I'll turn liquid and pour over top of you."
But she's already asleep. He strokes the inside
of her ankles and thinks of the peaks of roofs,
and eating malted milk balls Christmas morning,
of a new car, 58 miles on its odometer,
an evening of open road, an orange tinted sky.

## The Distance of Motion

I've fallen in love with a balding man
who's reading a book on the subway
into town. I can't see the title,
and really the man's just decent-looking—
with wire-rimmed glasses pressed hard
to his face, his nearly hairless head,
soft fuzz on the sides or maybe
bristle (I'd like to run my hands
across and see). I love, though, his lips,
the way he moves them to the words
like a five-year-old learning to read.
I'd guess this fellow's at least 40,
a tall, slender, still enthralled reader,
coaxing the words out of the pages,
as if he wants to taste this language,
not just scan the font some book designer
in New York chose months or years ago.
I watch him through six stops. I see
he wears no ring. But now this man,
this would-be-future-husband's rising,
stepping onto the platform outside,
his book closed, lips pressed tight,
the light outside too bright, glancing
off the windows of nearby houses,
the fenders of parked cars, the top
of the man's head. Everywhere's shining
like polished glass now, as the engines
kick in, the wheels screech, and we hurtle
again down seamless steel tracks.

## Wheels Inside Wheels

It's not so easy, the next man,
the warmth of his hands
against my body, the moist impress
of his kiss, defining me apart
from you, from that night
you cried up into me—
moments like that turning
to simply moments like that.
I think of you in pieces: a blue eye,
flush of the cheek, those nights
we lay naked on my bed, you
like a mouth sucking at my heart.
Now at night I reach for him,
hanging hard like he's the slender rope,
the frozen water stretching below,
and love's illusive, a gesture
glimpsed from the corner of the eye,
a breath against an earlobe.

## If Only

If only we were always beginning to love,
my trembling need, your hands warm
pressing my back, my sides, your lips
everywhere changing me. If only I
could keep it so, I'd hold you in that
pose of open tenderness, something
of your face at once desiring and content
as if what your eyes had strained to find
at last fell on the thing. If only I could
always feel so rightly placed, my body
lovely because you name it so, your fingers
making me willing, supple, graced.

## Winter Preparations

I find you nailing up the framing boards,
mixing the cement. You work each time
I leave. I come back, there's another course
of brick. The drywall's leaning against a tree.
You smile with a look that says, pay no
attention. You don't want me to speak,
just feel—feel. You close my eyes with kisses
("it's nothing"), carry me down to where the sun
makes a jagged pool between the shadows.
I lie adrift, pretending it might be safe.

I can convince myself of anything.
Later, the memory of sunlight grows cool.
Some wayward frogs hop across my porchstep.
The cabernet looks purple, and I press
a filled glass to my forehead. Below my feet,
the lake rises steadily. I know
you are out there sizing two by fours,
pounding another shingle to the roof.

## Moving Topsoil and Thinking about Us

By midday, my hands blister,
ache. My back feels as if a team
of Clydesdales has stumbled
over top of it. In every shovelful,
rocks—sometimes rocks the size
of human heads—emerge. I find
bits of glass, a marble, a plastic tractor,
a brass doorknob. Each item
means another kind of work.
Homer, the man who brought the load,
said, "It's good topsoil. Straight
from outta the earth." Sticks, roots,
dead grass. I'm at it all day shoveling,
hauling, picking out the refuse as I move
one pile, to another pile, to another.

# The Edge of Enough

## I. Wood

Not a deer, but the shadow of a deer
steps through trees. Not love
but the shadow of it, his hand
passing across my face, the words
he puts in my mouth like pieces
of ripe fruit: "complex," "passive,"
"sonorous," I could chew on
for hours, but he's tired, anxious,
his body moves above me as heavy
as wool drenched in pond water.
I can almost embrace hooves—
become mud, pine needles, fern.

## II. Water

Almost touched in the place
he fears the most, he swims
ahead of me. I am nearly drowning.
His feet scissor-kick through a green froth
of sunlight, bubbles, dirt fragments—
pale legs dancing before me
like two strange angels—so beautiful
I keep stretching out toward, toward.
Not love but its shadow, enough
to spur my arms to reach again,
almost enough to split me
open, spiral, weightless, gone.

## En Route

I wanted to ride up 6th Avenue
in that sleek black cab forever,
head tucked against your chest,
fingers clutching your shirt's
soft flannel, our driver: wheel
in one hand, phone in the other,
weaving past limos and parked cars
and shouting in a language I didn't
recognize—you laughed, said
probably arguing about what to order
on the pizza—the lights of Manhattan
a gold shimmer streaming past,
a parade of couples hurrying
down the sidewalk, exhaling
clouds, and me, still with you,
warm and breathless, falling.

## Nowhere Fast

You left me waiting in that truck for hours.
I couldn't fall asleep. It was so hot
I think even the dashboard sweated. My head
an awkward lump against the armrest, I thought
of women all across the states, stuck
inside their mobile homes, their limousines,
their hotel rooms, some drinking beer, some crying,
some dressed in housecoats—singing country music
as they waltzed alone. One woman might
be talking on the phone, her heels kicked off
her nylons on the floor. The lady
sitting at the bar might drink her whiskey
neat. We'd all be waiting for a man
(different clothes, same damn story). Hearts,
near broken up with love, we might wait
a life while he's out drinking, or clinching
some big deal. You were my life, I thought.
Years I'd wait before I learned. But that's
another story. Not this one, which only
points to you—your sweating truck
a symbol of a man who keeps his woman
free but trapped, a man who's going
nowhere fast, his woman right there with him.

## Me and You and an Oh

My back against the bookcase,
your tongue on my ear, my foot

lifted to a shelf. You nearly shout,
sure you should stop, look down,

*Please,* I tell you with my eyes,
love that you know how to make me

always move when, *Shouldn't,*
*start that, but yes,* I add,

you say, *guilty, I'm nothing,* your
hands down my belly, dear

Jesus, but how to help how we,
like tissue between us, brush aside so easy.

It's just me then and you and an Oh.

## Hands Full of Nothing

The hotel lobby, a one-legged man
flops down next to me. I'm so tired
I could curl beside the fountain,
Cupid in its center, vomiting green water.
You were just on the phone, saying,
*I'd like to kneel down in front of you,*
*my tongue between your* . . . If I were there,
you wouldn't even take me out
to get a sandwich. The one-legged man
makes his living playing bass. His laugh
sounds like a horse. I close my eyes.
*I'd like to* . . . If I were there, you wouldn't even
meet me for a drink. Why do I call?
Here by nine, I drove through the night,
sunroof open, the sky a pincushion of stars.
To stay awake, I kept reaching up my hand
to grab, one more time, a fistful of wind.

# Letter, March 18

By now you have arrived home,
leafed through your mail, heard
the messages on your machine.

You have emptied your bag,
thrown your worn laundry
down the chute. You have changed.

Dark, pressed, you have backed
from your drive, the front porchlight
glancing yellow against the walkway.

By now you have arrived at the opera
and you sit on red, padded chairs,
beside her. By now the hotel bed sheets

have been replaced, the bed remade,
and someone else might lie there.
He touches her face, or she his,

or maybe they're watching CNN,
or he is thinking about the arc
of hills they just drove through,

or she is thinking about the sound
the rain makes against a rooftop.
By now I have pulled the blinds,

and the birds aren't singing,
and the train outside shrills: "Ohhh—oh."
And though it is still winter,

the crocuses in my yard are blooming purple.
And though it is still winter,
I can almost taste the heat.

## No News Here

I'm covered in cat hair, my arms,
my shoulders, and everybody knows
how I loved you, your head, your body,

your ringed finger. I thought
she was a friend. I told her, keep, don't,
this is mine: story, man, love, secret.

The thin gray lines on a page blur. I hear
she was drinking one night and said,
and now it's everywhere. But who am I

to be news—diet trends, a boy birthed
as half an orangutan, we can prevent
heart attacks by sucking on daisy petals—

and I am not news. My heart, rent,
might be pasted in a book, just like
everyone's—we're all broken

lovers, or we're sleepwalking.
What story do they hope to hear:
our bodies entwined on the bed,

then the slats bending through,
the mattress lurching awkwardly
to the floor? This is the way

the stars shift. This is the way headlights
burst into brightness, and this is the way I
get through my days: not very well.

# Returns

At the office, he starts to touch her
the way he does, but this time

she tries to say no, but how can she
say no when her body, his breath, his

need, her need, my god—
how can she? She's crying, he's saying,

*I love you, love you,* she can't see, just
bright lights, fingers melting her,

but this time, she tells him in her head,
*wrong, I can't do this, not anymore,*

*too hard—I'm so hard,*
she hears, all tangled up, wants to go,

stay, just be quiet in his arms,
when a knock on the door, and he,

*Can you go out the back?*
and she thinks, *It's her, it's her,*

and runs, leaves her sweater, her book,
leaves so fast she gets lost, and she's running

up and down the backstairs of his building
looking for an exit. Finally, she's out,

out and driving, thinking, *I'm lost,*
*I'm scared, I'm out of my mind.*

when a phone booth, quick, just to
hear him—she pulls over, frantically

digs between the seats for loose change.

## Common Dreams

I'm under their bed. I make a mad dash
for the door. Then a dark alley, and she's
on the chase, asthmatic rasping pant in my ears.

I'm crouched in her basement
tucked under the utility sink
when she opens the door, shining a flashlight.

The children are playing in the living room,
and I'm spying through the window.
When she enters the room and catches my eye,

her tray of cookies and milk goes flying,
and I'm off, darting between houses,
ducking into some junked-out car.

## The Mistress

You awaken from nightmares
in which you've seen her clearly.

She passed you on the street
and clucked at your little baby.

She held your bag of groceries
while you fumbled for your keys.

Then you turned, and she was gone,
your purse lost, your children screaming.

You imagine her treacherous, slick,
waiting under beds, or behind open doors.

Your hands make fists in the air.
Look closely in the mirror

and perhaps you'll see her face. Younger,
troubled, she is a version of you. Kiss her,

she smells humid and ivory. Press your palm
against her cheek and you are one.

## To One Who Can't Leave

From here to death may be a long road,
so stay with your wife.

Get home and be grateful.
The closet is waiting, ready for your coat.

Your children need you
to teach them the ways not to love.

Keep them safe with well-wrought lies.
Each child must have a sickness to grieve.

Let your loneliness be theirs.
They will know, you've managed for them.

It can be their slow guilt
as they climb you like rungs to the world.

## The Wish

In this cabin ants crawl across a shiny
hardwood floor. He doesn't seem to notice,
but all I can think of is their dirty legs

scuttling across my feet. Saturday, a cool
June morning in Vermont, Chet Baker
singing, "Whenever I fall in love

it's always you," except you're eight hundred
miles away attending a swim meet, a birthday party,
maybe daydreaming of a long late morning,

me beside you, the scent of daffodils
trickling through the windows.
Nothing is simple, not me or you

or even this sunny morning with the ants
scurrying back and forth and him
echoing loudly from the shower:

"It's *all-ways you,*" a song I'm certain
I'll always remember with the same sick
feeling in my gut. You said I'd betray you

at a moment's notice, as if you were standing
at the edge of a field humble and alone,
a farmer's hat in your hands, and I thumbing

my nose in New Orleans red dress, tiara,
man on each arm. "What do you want from me?"
your favorite phrase. I wanted the vacuum

no one lives in: you beside me,
free and alone, your hand on my knee—
an endless, open stretch of road.

## Alone, Open Road

It was raining, a slow, persistent
December rain, the drops more like cold oil
than water as they spattered my face,
and the man by the roadside, held up

one Christmas tree after another.
All of them huge, I said, "I don't know.
I don't know. What about that one?"
"You'll have to get your husband

to trim it down for you." Usually I just smile,
nod, but this time, I admitted, "There's no
husband." Maybe I wanted to prove something.
He was short, dark-haired, greasy-looking,

with dirt-stained overalls and an orange coat
he wore unzipped. His eyes kind of bulged,
like creatures I've dissected in past
science experiments. I wondered if those were

blood-stains on his chest. "You're single?
What do you do?" "I teach." "You
want to go out sometime?" He paused.
"I bet you never dated a tree farmer."

An eighteen-wheeler careened past,
roar of wheels and water and engine.
I stared at my boots, wondered how
to get out of this one. "I'm Stan.

What's your name?" "Iris," I lied,
avoided his eyes. He shrugged,
hoisted the tree into my neighbor's pickup.
Back on the highway, I sang to the radio,

windshield wipers flapping, tree flouncing
in the truckbed. Sometimes it's not so bad,
traveling alone, open road, pedal to the floor.
No one to betray—no one to forgive.

# Friend of a Friend of a

We meet for brunch, and are seated beside a window.
Perching on sofas, which are awkwardly low,
we order sandwiches that come with misshapen
bits of greenery beside them on white plates.

When I take a bite, part of my sandwich is left
dangling from my mouth. He doesn't notice.
He's telling me about his company, rattling off initials:
A.C.E, I.C.A., and I don't know what else.

These are clients or businesses he's working for
or did work for. My friend told me he's smart,
that he's hoping to find a wife. We've only exchanged
e-mail before today. My date talks quickly,

and I strain to stay focused. I've been grading papers
all morning long. Outside: gray sky, a green car
chugging past. He pauses, "Am I boring you?"
"No, not at all. It's very interesting." And the man

keeps talking—about Canada's declining dollar.
He calls it a period of hangover after the party,
convalescence after the fever, because of debt,
and mismanaged trade agreements, "Who can say

when things will improve?" Somehow he links
this point to the American University, the way intelligence
is being sucked from even the poorest communities.
My coffee is cold. I smile, nod. It doesn't take much

to keep him going. "But now, tell me about
your own education?" I sum that up
in two or three sentences. What can I say
to a man with so many answers? It's pouring now.

Rain glazes the window, and a squat fellow
in a trench coat scurries past, newspaper over his head.
In one of his e-mails, he'd mentioned a late sister.
I ask. At once he becomes human, sad.

He had a sister who was also his business associate,
roller dance partner. He'd just bought her her first car,
a sports coupe, lipstick red. Twenty-two, she had
bleach-blonde hair, a chic cut, and an attitude.

She weighed only a hundred pounds.
Her hobbies were men, drinks, haute cuisine.
"We were close," he tells me. She was driving
home to the farm, but a careless neighbor hadn't

latched his gate. Clipping along fast, she couldn't stop
when she saw his horses in the road. One rolled
over top of her car, several others struck the front.
He passed the wreck, he said, didn't even know

it was her, her new coupe, a crunch of metal
in a ditch, the police directing traffic around
horse bodies. "It tore the fabric of my family
apart, but it's water under the bridge." The clichés—

how we need them. He is broken, just trying
to weave through the maze, as we all are.
The waitress is stacking chairs on tables; but the man
keeps talking till they turn out the overhead lights.

Outside, we stand beside his car. He's going on now
about the secession of Montreal, though it's raining again,
and I'm ready to get back to the rest of my student papers,
papers about significant events that have changed

these freshmen's lives. The students write:
"And now I know I'm not immortal," or
"I try to tell the ones I love the way I feel."
I write, "Weak Ending," or "Go Further,"

as if my own conclusions have been any better,
the man now driving off into a furrowed brow
of sky, the sound of wet tires against asphalt.

## Soul Mate

Mine is lost, poor dear.

## With a Woman

The dark openings of O'Keefe's flowers
loom large, when I look at the teen's face.
She explains in detail her boyfriend's
latest betrayals. I nod, nod again. It is easy
to feign sympathy. What of my tongue
against the petals? What of wet pollen
clinging to my fingertips? Afternoons,
young boys race past my window,
their bodies lithe, muscular, and yesterday,
the slender brisk man behind the deli counter
smiled like he wanted something. Easy
to think the lights dim when my wrist
bumps another, easy to grow warm, the wet
leaves of the rubber plant glistening
with spray, the cat purring, kneading my chest.
How would it be to turn the girl's fine-boned
face toward mine, press my hand to her cheek?
How would I slide down where there are
no sure handles, only warm dark spaces
that soften and open to take another in?

## Teaching Composition in Erie, Pennsylvania, or Madonna Should Never Write a Dating Column

I'm trying to write a funny poem about Madonna,
about an interview the star granted recently with a Hungarian
who kept asking her about her sex life.
The interviewer, for instance, asks Madonna,
"When you met Carlos, were you dating
many other people in your bed at the same time?
And what was your book 'Slut' about?"
(The actual book title, you may remember, is *Sex*.
and I wonder: does sex equal slut in Hungaria?)
The Hungarians, says her interviewer, like to hear
her musical productions and "move their bodies in response."
He asks if she's "a bold hussy-woman
that feasts on men who are tops."
"Yes, yes," she affirms, but she is "a woman,
not a test mouse." It's winter in Erie, capitol of antidepressants.
My poem comes out like a mix between a cookbook recipe
and a textbook assignment. I try it rhyming.
But what rhymes with Madonna? Lasagna?
You wanna? How about Hungarian? Librarian?
I'm wearing him? I scrawl: "I'm a woman, not a test mouse.
Put your fingers on my dress blouse." It's not funny
that it's been gray in town for weeks, that I spend my time
reading poorly constructed sentences when I chose
to study literature for the love of good writing.
And besides, my body, dying to be touched,
hates Madonna, whose men trail after her
like dogs following a steak, who is not being ironic when she says,
"In America it is not considered mentally ill when a woman
advances on her prey in a discotheque setting with cocktails."
I'd sooner kiss a toilet than go to a discotheque,
but even my grandmother's giving me dating advice:
"What about joining a gym? I hear you can meet
nice young men that way." I sit at home
imagining the five single men in Erie

with long nasal hairs and halitosis, or pale and doughy
selling fake wood furniture at Value City,
which is unfair and ridiculous, but my therapist tells me,
it's okay, I'm exploring new dimensions of myself.
Well, new dimensions have done nothing
for my social life. And writing this poem
about Madonna, who's obviously having
way more sex than I am, is just depressing.

## Winter, Erie, PA

Once I knelt beside the barn mid-January.
My fingers were shaking
and white as bleached bone.
I was trying to catch hold

of something. I couldn't see
what it was. I must have wanted it
bad though. I kept putting them back
into the snow, pulling them out.

I thought: *something important*
*is happening here.* But it was cold,
and no one came to touch me
on the shoulder. Standing, my horse

dozed in his stall. I was twelve.
I was hungry. I believed what I felt.
But that was a long time ago.
Maybe it means nothing to you.

Still, when you ask me how I am,
I think of the fingers reaching out,
reaching out, then coming back,
empty and still so very cold.

## I Believe in Pain the Way Others Believe in God

*for M.O.*


*I don't experience God,*
says Michael, his cheeks glowing
in the café's weak light. *I think*
*I will always be lonely,*
he tells me. As we talk,
I can't piece his face together.
I see him the way Picasso painted
the woman wearing a hat,
all angles and fragments.
My hands look thin, and I think
I might be slowly disappearing.
He says, *I go into a crowded room*
*and feel all the pain.* I wonder,
does God make a noise we can't hear?
I worry about this friend of mine,
who is quiet, sad. I'd ask God,
Do you like holding us
by the throat? Michael asks,
*How can people live with all that pain?*
Later, a shabby man
clutching a bottle of whiskey
crosses in front of my car.
There's a stoplight, a woman
inside a building, practicing
piano. It's so easy to get confused:
driving, stopping to buy milk,
then I look up, and it's raining,
and my flight from Detroit
to New Orleans has landed.
Factories dim behind gumbo
and Dixieland, and I'm donning
several strings of beads, one white,
one blue, one violet, like in a postcard
for tourists, but I'm not smiling
standing beside a park bench,
a statue of a soldier missing an arm.

## Lyric Melancholia in Winter

Leave me alone with your happiness.
I want none of your banners
and sombreros, plates of spaghetti
heaped to the chandeliers.
What of the maimed bird
circling to the damp? What of the
starvelings' scaffold of bones?
In the evening, a damned man
pulls at his hair, shrieks:
"Aye! Aye! Aye! Aye!"
They will run to him, the people
who run to others, in their nun's
clothes, and their white coats.
They will put their hands
on his sleeves. They will
shush him. They are just
doing their jobs. Outside,
the sun is an orange bulb
half-hidden by trees. Then,
it is the memory of orange.
Down the hall, the shy girl
who cleans the lavatories
will be pulling on her coat.
Her mother is waiting
with toast and tea, and always
the same questions: *How
was your day? Did you eat?*
Perhaps it snows. Perhaps
a policeman is smoking
on a nearby city street.
He leans against a lamppost,
takes a long, slow drag.
You should imagine
the piss-soaked leaves,
the steam of the manholes,
the damp, graveyard smell
rising through iron grates.

## The Letter I Sent To My Mother

is not the one I should have sent.
I wrote, though it's still winter,
it no longer snows.
I work too hard.
Something you said when we last spoke
made me think of a constellation
in the form of a bread basket.
Sometimes, I miss home,
Dad drinking whiskey on the couch,
you wearing oven mitts,
the house smelling of roast beef.

I didn't say that mothers are arms
stretching open to spread a towel
or the face of a flower lifted
to a nose, how my uncle
kissed me hard on the mouth
the night I babysat
after my aunt made me cry,
and I was still crying,
tasting whiskey, stumbling
up the driveway from his car.
Or the lake yesterday,
so gray and still it looked like stone.
If I were Jesus, I would have
walked on it. Anything
to make her understand.

## Explanations for Distraction

Because the refrigerator is full
of bruised home-grown tomatoes,
because she's tired, and her cats
howl for no reason,
and the blue nose of the sky
is sniffing the sidewalk,
and she's hot, and the neighbor
is clipping hedges
into shapely women's hips,
and because this winter
will be long and cold,
hornets building their nests
near the ground, while the moon
tucks its chin
shyly behind clouds,
and the maples rattle impatiently.
And he waits, still,
but she's washing the dishes, or sighing,
staring out the window
at the accumulating Hemlock needles,
maybe wishing west—her heart flown
like laundry from the line:
a nightgown headed for the hills,
a crisp white shirt, a man's chest,
burly with wind,
dancing above a lamppost.

## Her Power

*for Uncle Jim, home brewer,*
*lover of pints*

She wants you—can you see that?—
lips wet, body moist with anticipation.
She was even shaking—
did you notice?—when she
heard your heavy step across the floor.
Reach over. Put your hand
against her hips. Feel the cool
hard curve of her. You can
take her as you might
a handful of rose petals,
sweet succulence rising to your lips.
Or grab her fast and rough as you would
the steering wheel on a truck.
Don't let her rigid exterior deceive you.
She aims to please. Vibrant,
amber, she can teach you
all the right moves. Lie back.
Let her pour through you
like heat. Feel yourself
relax. She knows the way
to open and soothe you. Don't
resist. You deserve this attention.
No matter the high-rises, envelopes,
and taxicabs of your mind.
You're under her power now.
You're not going anywhere.

## The Art of Schmoozing

The art of schmoozing isn't hard to master.
You have to tell yourself: this isn't lonely,
but fun, chatting up the boss half-plastered,

or watching men with shiny foreheads cluster
around the slinky babe. Enjoy the phony
laughs, the posing. It isn't hard to master

the elbow leaned against a wall, the gesture
to a passing friend, listening vaguely
to a bore who's going on half-plastered.

Keep your distance. Watch the small disasters:
botched names, ignored crushes, snubs, it's any
voyeur's paradise, so easy to master.

Even a dismal party has its luster:
its damp face, tipped glass, lively crony
perched beside the fireplace half-plastered.

When the hostess appears be sure to toast her,
Remember to smile, be gracious, nod. Clearly,
the art of schmoozing isn't hard to master,
although it's easier to take half-plastered.

## My Former Lover Said He Was Tired

I think how late last night
he must have rocked her
in his tarnished brass bed,
his body lodged in her body
and breaking into spasms,
delirious, hot with longing
they cried, voices broken,
emerging in odd intervals
the way a paper airplane falls
from the sky, first gliding, then
swerving, then nose-diving
from the rooftop, down to the river,
where a lone duck circles,
and a dark, leafless tree
leans across from the opposite shore,
its branches a black tapestry
cast eerily across the water,
which moves purposely,
unwearying, and never slows,
and carries whatever is light
to some cool, shadowy end.

## What's Left

No wonder women love him.
When I'd go out of town,
he wouldn't sleep in our bed.
Those nights, he'd sit in the dark
watching T.V., blanket pulled
to his chin. No wonder,
weeks after our parting—
him sobbing as he backed
out the driveway in his jeep—
he curled inside another's arms,
then later wept, telling me. It was fall;
the hemlocks in the backyard
dropped needles so fast I swept up
a garbage bag full each week.

A confessor, he described
how they'd met: the bar dimly-lit,
their talk of abstract art, the kiss
beside her car. He told me, *I still
love you.* No wonder I felt nauseous
for days. Those hemlocks that year,
a plague, dry sheath of needles drowning
my shuffleboard square of a lawn.
I found them in the cat's bowl,
on the dining table, jabbing
at my ankles through my socks.
He was in grad school, states away.
I stared down a month of nights,
swept pine until my hands were raw.

## What We Keep When Lovers Go

The tulips he sent me are dead.
I leave them in the vase,

my table strewn with fuchsia petals,
all curled and dry. And from the stems,

what used to be concealed emerges:
tiny white phalluses, miniature shafts

with bulbous heads, pricks,
properly-sized for mice or birds,

hidden before like thoughts of sex
beneath a friendly smile, a hard-on

under a woolen kilt. For days
I let stand the bald, naked,

rotting stalks with their penile ends,
nubs I might run my finger across,

but don't. Why do I keep them,
the plants' green leaves grown limp,

the water in the vase a fetid,
brown soup? Is it nostalgia—the thought

of his thought of me? Or is it sex
after all? How quickly we slip back

into ourselves, him gone to wherever
lovers go, these flowers a memento.

# The Feeling of Wings

*for Tom Judd*

The faces of past lovers
fly in and out of her heart
like the shadows of blackbirds
skimming across a pond,
and his fingers twined
between hers as they lie
side by side like siblings
help her know she is alive
but still caught on the edges
of the impossible, like a monarch
caught in the dry web
of a dead spider. No one
to drink from her, no one
to set her free. She sees it the way
the almost-dead have seen
their bodies down below them,
the pale naked skin of the neck,
the unfluttering eyelids cool
as November, the tongue
thick with hidden defeat.
She must learn again the feeling
of wings, brilliant yellow burning
from her shoulders, the passion
of wind—the glorious gasp.

## After the Goodbye

First we creep past the platform,
a long black scarf blown across
a woman's face, a man shaking his umbrella,
a row of trench coats, mealy-toned, dour.
Beyond the station, the sky is gray,
the landscape muted. Here, two boys
shove each other on the sidewalk.
There, a small, black poodle, a killer,
lunging and barking ferociously.

Now trees puff past. A white church
braces its heels, balancing steeply
on a hillside. Dreamy, they go,
and they go, and I am there too
inside the rush, my body lost in the hills,
the herd of cows musing beside a sycamore,
the birds circling on their slick wheels.

## Ars Poetica

I should go now beyond the barn
where inside, horses snort and mouth
strands of hay, beyond the fence line,
beside which tall thin weeds barely peek
above the snowbank, where I'll sink
to my thighs, where the field lies
covered and white and gentle,
and it is quiet as death. Further back,
where the treeline begins and the land
drops down, the creek's still moving,
its lining of fallen leaves not quite frozen,
its movement sending steam into the still
and frigid air. If I crouch there
on top of the snow, my knees
sunk, blue jeans into whiteness, will I know?
If I take off my gloves and thrust
my hands into the water, will I know?
I should go further than the stream
back into the woods, where the snow
is shallower, but blown in piles
against the tree trunks. I should try
to stop shaking. I should remember
the barn, the warm moist nostrils of the horses.
I should press on until nothing
looks familiar, but all is similar: thin
trunks of trees and beneath them
the snow making miniature landscapes
of hills and valleys, a whistling
from somewhere, and cold, a little
bit frightened, I should stop again
and listen again, until I start to know.

## Boardwalk and Bach

Old man in a sweatered-blue slouch
on the only nearby bench,
his scant strands of hair
combed hopefully over his scalp,
while cormorants circle the shoreline,
and beyond them, straining
to ride the wind, a kite,
four-cornered, tail snapping
like a mad cat's. A violin's
arm of ache haunts my Toyota,
in front of which a moth-eaten dog,
black, squat, red-eyed and jowly,
thrusts his head into the garbage.
But it isn't just the way the dog finds a bag,
pulls it out, nuzzles it gently,
then tears it with his teeth,
licks the inside carefully, almost tenderly,
nor how the old man eats his sandwich,
withered hands trembling,
stained with blotches. It is all of us,
sitting in our cars near the boardwalk
or waiting in line for a hotdog,
or pulling on our sweatshirts.
*Where are you going? Where are you going?*
The violin sobs. The day tucks up
into itself and trundles inward. Still we stay.
Here the man, there the dog, the kite,
the little girl walking past,
pink-dressed, her patent leather shoes,
her chewing gum, her hand in the hand
of a tall man wearing a suit.
The dog lifts its leg. Waves slash
again and again against the shore.

## Again

the leaves on the maple are crimson;
the old wooden swing out back
looks tired; and the boys, swearing,
wheel past on their bicycles; again
they are trying to prove who they are.
Again the postman looks distracted
walking his route, and the wind
howls against my house like an imitation
ghost in a B movie. We are backing
from the driveway, and the lawn
needs mowed, and the boys on bicycles
are not the same boys, but they say
the same things: "Your mother," "Kiss mine."
Again we don't know what to eat,
and the cat is rubbing against our shin,
or the damn dog is barking, and again,
even though the trees are at their peak—
indigo and burgundy, apricot and peach—
the sky seems faded. Even though love
is possible, the faces look pale.
Even though beauty breaks our hearts,
so does the stick rattling across the asphalt,
so does the old grocer, shaving off
the perfect piece of ham. How frail
he looks holding it up to the light
to show the thickness, then wrapping it
carefully, carefully sliding it into the bag.

## Matin

Silent morning spread across a city
in arcs of light, and lampposts and
rooftops quietly assert themselves,
a fluff of squirrel
leaps along a telephone wire,
and a postman leaves his house
with hat askew, and birds
have found a loaf of bread
torn up and thrown on the ground,
and the feast is more than they can bear:
they scream and dive and peck,
and you, still sleeping, stretched
long across our poster bed, soft,
soft sleep there, because
white sheets at a cheek,
and the glass of orange juice
held in our neighbor's hand
are enough for now, simply enough.

## Worms Dancing

Just last week it snowed. The shroud of winter
for months has hung above our roofs like oil,
but now blossoms dot the yard with color.
Lemon, orange, and red, they spring from the soil
like children in brightly colored shirts bursting
from under blankets. One neighbor's already out
and poking in her yard, coiffed hair, blue
knickers hiking toward her knees. Here come
some boys on bikes across the lawn, they shout
and land on only one wheel, skid toward home.
They're crazy with the knot of sex that's thrusting
from every bough and petal, so thick and new
that even the worms emerge from dirt and shit
to writhe and double from the thrill of it.

## My Doggy Self

*after Lynn Emanuel, who
compares her reader to a dog*

I am no longer the dog at the end
of your leash, which, you must admit,
you kept jerking, choking me,
and another thing, you dragged me away
from that sweet-smelling hydrant
to look at that woman in a red dress,
who I didn't like anyway, hair teased
and sprayed into a cloud around her head.
She was the kind who habitually
gives a friendly dog a knee to the chest.
There you were erasing all the stuff
that elated me: the grin of the moon,
the sleek elbow of the street, the lamplight
pooling on the ground in a greasy,
oblong, golden smear. I wanted
everything: brown turds fragrant
as raw meat, the open bag of garbage—
white paper wrapper slicked with fish juice,
cigar stubs, used Kleenex, pantyhose
with a run in the crotch. Meanwhile,
you kept tearing me away: first
from the hydrant, then the red dress,
then the armor of a trench coat.
You know how I like to linger, my long
readerly snout buried in the armpit
of the trench coat, my body stretched
across the sun-warmed sidewalk.
What snippet of voice could give me
such pleasure? What blank page?

## Audience of Two

The couple is in love. They sit
hand in hand, the only two
audience members aside from my host.
She's lovely, young, blonde,
her hair pulled back, her smile
immediate. He's dark-haired,
pretty, a bit tousled. They are students,
they tell me, and writers of poetry.
The work I read is cynical and witty,
all pieces about failed or failing
relationships. The couple listens,
leans forward nodding. After,
they come up shyly and thank me.
Later, I spy them kissing in a corner.
They don't believe the admonitions.
Why should they? Wherever they go
the air around them shimmers.

## When Can I See Your Shetland Ponies,

their muzzles twitching, bashful eyes
hidden behind thick forelocks,
like grade school girls, quiet and shy,
solemn behind thick bangs? When
can I wrap their necks in my arms, scratch
the tender spot behind their ears, bask
dreamy in your sun-swept paddock,
where a flock of hens pecks through strands
of hay, where the one you saved scolds—
wings on her hips—if their dish goes
empty? When will you show me the roses
you've bred and tended, your gloved hands
clipping back overgrown sprigs, then
gathering withered blossoms into a bowl?

## Pilgrimage

We make our way to this park, the end
of Lincoln Ave, this patch of well-coifed grass:
me, the couple in khakis, their hands buried
in each other's back pockets,
the man on a bicycle, some teens
shivering in T-shirts, their brown lab
snuffling at the end of his leash.
Below us the bay: shifting, impatient;
the boathouse with its sailboats leaning
elegantly to one side. Meanwhile,
the sun's peach eye sinks quickly
toward the bay's-edge. A man
holding a blue coffee cup stands to my left.
A woman huffs to the curb
pushing a baby carriage. We are silent,
shifting foot to foot. White smudged lines
of an airplane crisscross above the sun,
whose bottom has melted now
into the water's lap. A green Porsche
slowly cruises past. A bird hovers above us
then dives, and the sun's a pale half
dollar in a yowl of plum and scarlet.
How the sky seems to reel with it then:
that heft of fire descending, now copper,
now chartreuse, now a darkened
smear of gold, and we're dumb, straining,
lingering to the end, when we will turn
back into strangers, but now, transfixed,
we are one eye burning with glory.

CPSIA information can be obtained
at www.ICGtesting.com
Printed in the USA
LVHW090350240221
679762LV00002B/34

9 780814 257234